With

to A

Marcia

Isle of Iona, 5/23/06

MAKER'S BLESSING

Prayers and meditations
from the Iona Community

WILD GOOSE PUBLICATIONS

Prayers/meditations © the individual contributors
Compilation and design © Wild Goose Publications

First published 2000 by Wild Goose Publications
4th Floor, Savoy House, 140 Sauchiehall Street,
Glasgow G2 3DH, UK
Reprinted 2005

Wild Goose Publications is the publishing division of
the Iona Community. Scottish Charity No. SCO03794.
Limited Company Reg. No. SCO96243.

ISBN 1 901557 24 3

Cover and page design by Wild Goose Publications

A catalogue record for this book is available
from the British Library.

Distributed in Australia by Willow Connection Pty Ltd,
Unit 7A, 3-9 Kenneth Road, Manly Vale, NSW 2093,
Australia. Permission to reproduce any part of this work
in Australia or New Zealand should be sought from
Willow Connection.

Produced by Reliance Production Company, Hong Kong.
Printed and bound in China.

MAKER'S BLESSING

MAY THE MAKER'S BLESSING BE YOURS

May the Maker's blessing be yours
encircling you round
above you
within you

May the Son's blessing be yours
the wine and the water
the bread and the stories
to feed you
to remind you

May the Spirit's blessing be yours
the wind, the fire
the still small voice
to comfort you
to disturb you

May the angels' blessing be yours
and the joy of the saints

to inspire you
to cherish you

And may my own blessing be yours
a blessing rooted
in our common pilgrimage
the blessing of a friend.

GOD OF LIGHT
AND WARMTH

O God, star kindler
kindle a flame of love within us
to light our path in days of darkness

O God, sun warmer
warm us with your love
to melt the frozen hand of guilt

O God, moon burnisher
burnish the shield of faith
that we may seek justice
and follow the ways of peace

GOD, OUR PASSIONATE LIFE

God, our passionate life
we bless you for the infinite beauty
of created things

sand, wind, wave
and the wings of the eagle

for the love of land and people
for the vine and the fruit
and the good wine

We bless you
for the endurance of hope
for the promise of renewal
and for fleeting moments
on the mountaintop

Blessed are you,
God our passionate life

But if we have forgotten those
who bear the marks of exile,
desert, home,
upon their hands and feet
and suffer them to go on bleeding

if we have dismembered
the body of God

have mercy on us,
God who brings us down to earth
ground us in justice
root us in right relationship
give flesh to our words and worship
with the breath and peace of your spirit
until joy is our only, holy common ground
Amen

LITANY OF LETTING GO

I let go:
window and door
house and home
memory and fear.

I let go the hurt of the past
and look to the hope of the future.

I let go
knowing that I will always carry
part of my past (part of you) with me
woven into the story of my life.

Help me, Christ my brother
to softly fold inside
the grief and the sadness,
to pack away the pain
and to move on;
taking each day in your company;
travelling each step
in your love.

GOD OF LIFE

God of the past
who has fathered and mothered us
we are here to thank you

God of the future
who is always ahead of us
we are here to trust you

God of the present
here in the midst of us
we are here to praise you

God of life
beyond us within us
we rejoice in your glorious love

IN THE SILENCE

When the world tells us
we are what we do
with our activity, acumen
or achievement
let us learn
we are what we do with our silence

When the world tells us
we are what we do with
our spending power, selling power,
or our power of speech
let us learn
we are what we do with our silence

When the world tells us
to drown the silent sufferings of others
with indifference or noise
or to forget the art of stillness
even in the storm
let us learn
we are what we do with our silence

Where the world tells us
to rush in where angels fear to tread
let us learn that angels listen first
before they take a step
for the voice of God in the silence ...

RAG AND BONE CONFESSION

There are lumps under our carpet
that the hoover won't help

There are cats tied in bags
would be off like a flash

Skeletons in the cupboards
tap tap on the doors

There is nothing hidden
but that's going to get out
So let's get it over with, God

There's a pile at the foot of the cross
of the things we could do without

Make us glad we brought them
to you who carry away
the sins of the world
and grant in their place
pardon and grace
and your call to be following always.

THE CUP

We come, original clay to Your hand,
ready to be moulded to Your purpose,
wet with the living waters.

Humble, we submit to the power
of Your will,
we begin to spin into life.

Awry and out of balance,
we long for your centring touch
yet resist on first contact.

Full of the words and images
of the world,
we swing this way and that
till Your firm hand grasps us,
pulls us back,
draws us to the centre,
spinning into rings.

Yielding, we spin,
begin to sing,
picking up the rhythm,
rising and falling
becoming smooth
forming and filling.

Slowing, we spin,
vessel we become,
vessel to be shared,
full of the living waters.

LIGHT FOR LIFE

The sky does it simply, naturally
day by day by day
the sun does it joyfully
like someone in love
like a runner on the starting-line
the sky, the sun,
they just can't help themselves
no loud voices, no grand speeches
but everyone sees,
and is happy with them.

Make us like that, Lord
so that our faith is not in our words
but in our lives
not in what we say
but in who we are

passing on your love
like an infectious laugh:
not worried, not threatening,
just shining
like the sun,
like a starry night,
like a lamp on a stand,
light for life —
your light for our lives.

CIRCUIT

I make my circuit
in the fellowship of my God
on the machair, in the meadow,
on the cold heathery hill,
on the corner in the open,
on the chill windy dock,
to the noise of drills blasting,
to the sound of children asking.

I make my circuit
in the fellowship of my God
in city street
or on spring-turfed hill,
in shop-floor room
or at office desk.

God has no favourite places.
There are no special things.
All are God's and all is sacred.

I tread each day

in light or dark
in the fellowship of my God.

Be the sacred Three of glory
interwoven with our lives
until the Man who walks it with us
leads us home
through death to life.

MOVING HOUSE

When the removal men left,
table and chairs were still
out in the yard.
We had so many belongings —
far more than we needed.

Holy Spirit,
for whom there is room
in every home,
help to clear a way
through the clutter of possessions,
to make room for those who live there
to be fully themselves,
and for outsiders to be welcomed.

Spirit of hospitality, bless all
who share meals at our table –
even if it's still
out in the yard.

THE SHADOW OF THE DOVE

When dawn's ribbon of glory
around the world returns
and the earth emerges from sleep

May the shadow of the dove be seen
as she flies across moor and city.

Over the warm breast of the earth
she skims,
her shadow falling on
the watcher in the tower,
the refugee in the ditch,
the weary soldier at the gate.

May the shadow of peace
fall across the all-night sitting of a council
across the tense negotiators
around a table.

May the shadow of hope
be cast across the bars of a hostage cell

filling with momentary light
rooms tense with conflict,
bringing a brief respite,
a sliver of gold across the dark.

May she fly untiring
across flooded fields,
across a city divided by hate and fear,
across a town wreathed in smoke.

May the shadow of reconciliation,
the dove of peace
with healing in her wings,
be felt and seen and turned towards
as she makes righteousness shine
like the dawn,
the justice of her cause
like the noonday sun.

Holy Spirit of love
Bring healing, bring peace

HOW TERRIBLE

How terrible for us
when we ignore the presence of strangers

How terrible for us
when the sick and the old remain lonely

How terrible for us
when the little ones are hurt or ignored

How terrible for us
when the prisoner is deemed
beyond redemption or love

How terrible for us
when we do not question laws
that reward the strong
and put down the weak

How terrible for us
when we know what we should do,
and we walk the other way

How terrible for us,
for we bring God's anger upon ourselves
and we walk into outer darkness.

THOMAS

Put your hand,
Thomas,
on the crawling head
of a child
imprisoned
in a cot
in Romania.

Place your finger,
Thomas,
on the list of those
who have disappeared
in Chile.

Stroke the cheek,
Thomas,
of the little girl
sold in prostitution
in Thailand.

Touch, Thomas,
the gaping wounds
of my world.

Feel, Thomas,
the primal wound
of my people.

Reach out your hands,
Thomas,
and place them at the side of the poor.

Grasp my hands, Thomas,
and believe.

NEW WAYS

God of our lives
you are always calling us
to follow you into the future,
inviting us to new ventures,
new challenges,
new ways to care,
new ways to touch the hearts of all.

When we are fearful of the unknown,
give us courage.
When we worry
that we are not up to the task,
remind us that you would not call us
if you did not believe in us.

When we get tired,
or feel disappointed
with the way things are going,
remind us
that you can bring change and hope
out of the most difficult situations.

GOD OF STRANGENESS
AND DESIRE

God of strangeness and desire
we bless you for enticing us
to the last place we wanted to be
the place where we can hide no longer
where we must face
our own emptiness
and see our false gods fall.

We bless you
for the immeasurable relief
of self-exposure
for the miracle of survival
and for coming to us
in unexpected guises.

Blessed are you,
God of strangeness and desire.

But if we have turned in
upon our emptiness

refused the risks you require of us
idolised our self-sufficiency
and clung to our captivity

Have mercy on us,
God who wrestles and embraces us,
shatter our illusions
refuse your comfort of angels
feed our hope and our hunger
with the adventurous faith of your spirit
until grace is our only sufficiency
Amen

BIRTH

To wait
to endure
to be vulnerable
to accept
to be of good courage
to go on
day after day after day;
to be heavy with hope
to carry the weight of the future
to anticipate with joy
to withdraw with fear
until the pain overcomes
the waters break
and the light of the world
is crowned.
Then the travail is over
joy has overcome.

Lord of heaven and earth,
crowned with blood
at your birth,

delivered with pain,
bring new hope to birth
in your waiting world
bring fresh joy
to those who weep.
Be present
in all our dyings and birthings.

GOD BEYOND BORDERS

God beyond borders
we bless you for strange places
and different dreams

for the demands and diversity
of a wider world

for the distance
that lets us look back and re-evaluate

for new ground
where broken stems can take root,
grow and blossom.

We bless you
for the friendship of strangers
the richness of other cultures
and the painful gift of freedom

Blessed are you,
God beyond borders.

But if we have overlooked
the exiles in our midst
heightened their exclusion
by our indifference
given our permission
for a climate of fear
and tolerated a culture of violence

Have mercy on us,
God who takes side with justice,
confront our prejudice
stretch our narrowness
sift out our laws and our lives
with the penetrating insight
of your spirit
until generosity is our only measure.
Amen

WAITING

God, so much of faith is waiting

like a pregnant woman
waiting in hope

like a people under siege
holding out till relief comes

like the soul lost in the darkness
unable to see even a glimmer of light
yet stumbling through the night
because somewhere,
out ahead,
day will surely break

God, be with us in our waiting

THE WAY TO PEACE

Hiroshima,
Bosnia,
Belfast,
the names slip through our fingers
like bloodstained beads.

As we tell the story,
tell us,
tell us,
tell us,
the way
to peace.

Kosovo,
Nagasaki,
Nuremberg,
still they come,
countless numbers:
people hounded,
refugees tramping the road
out of hell, into hell.

Where will it stop?
Show us,
show us,
show us,
the way to peace.

Five for sorrow,
ten for joy.
May what has been sown in pain
be reaped in hope.

AS WINTER TREES

As winter trees
stretch out bare arms to a dark sky
we stretch out in the darkness
to find the touch of love

As snowdrops
turn their gentle faces to the sun
we long to find in that warmth
the promise of peace

As the fire
breaks the shell of the seed
so may our pain
break the shell of isolation
that protects us from ourselves

In the security of darkness
the warmth of sunshine
the promise of fire
may we blossom anew
in the miracle of your saving love, O God

THE LOVE OF THE FAITHFUL CREATOR

The love of the faithful Creator
The peace of the wounded Healer
The joy of the challenging Spirit
The hope of the Three in One
surround and encourage you
today, tonight and forever.

INDEX AND AUTHORS

Most of the prayers and meditations in this book have previously appeared in *The Pattern of Our Days*, a collection of liturgies and resources for worship. 'The Cup' is from *Dandelions and Thistles*. Both are published by Wild Goose Publications.

Wild Goose Publications is the publishing house of the Iona Community, an ecumenical Christian community founded in 1938 and committed to finding new ways of living the Gospel in today's world. With its original inspiration in the poorest areas of Glasgow during the Depression, the Community has sought ever since the 'rebuilding of the common life', bringing together work and worship, prayer and politics, and the sacred and the secular.

For more information about the Iona Community's work and its centres in Glasgow and on the Isle of Iona (Iona Abbey and the MacLeod Centre) and the Ross of Mull (Camas Adventure Camp), please contact:

The Iona Community, 4th Floor, Savoy House, 140 Sauchiehall Street, Glasgow G2 3DH, UK. Tel: 0141 332 6343   Fax: 0141 332 1090

For a catalogue of books, tapes and CDs produced by Wild Goose Publications, please contact:

Wild Goose Publications
(at the address above)
Tel: 0141 332 6292   Fax: 0141 332 1090
e-mail: admin@ionabooks.com
www.ionabooks.com